Pacific Grove

Architecture & Anecdotes

Dedicated to the community
of Pacific Grove

PUBLISHED BY

The BookWorks

667 Lighthouse Avenue,
Pacific Grove, CA 93950
www.bookworkspg.com

TEXT
Rebecca Riddell
Nell Flattery Carlson & Margot Tegtmeier

Copy Editor
Rena Henderson

PHOTOGRAPHY
Craig Riddell

HISTORIC PHOTOGRAPHS
Pat Hathaway's California Views

REFERENCE MATERIALS
Heritage Society of Pacific Grove
City of Pacific Grove
Archives from the Pacific Grove Tribune
Vintage House Book, by Tad Burness

Introduction

Pacific Grove, California is a tiny jewel of a town, rich in history and natural beauty. Perched on the very tip of California's Monterey Peninsula, it is surrounded on three sides by the Pacific Ocean and the Monterey Bay National Marine Sanctuary. Pacific Grove is famous for its Monarch butterflies, the striking purple carpet of ice plant that blooms along the coastline each spring, and the charming Victorian-era homes that line its streets.

Pacific Grove is nationally recognized as "America's Last Hometown," "The Most Romantic City In The USA," and "Butterfly Town, USA." Founded in the Victorian era, Pacific Grove's unique beginnings are still quite evident today through its architecture, which has been preserved and cherished by the community.

The city itself is geographically less than three square miles yet boasts over 1300 historic properties on its official Historic Register—more than any other city of its size on the West Coast. Many of its streetscapes reflect the city's architectural heritage.

This book is a small tribute to Pacific Grove's unique architecture and the history it conveys. A number of the featured properties have been rehabilitated for modern use in the 21st Century, while others have very few alterations. These structures have been photographed as they stood in 2016, many with worn paint and other signs of age.

The Pacific Grove Chamber of Commerce, assisted by the Heritage Society of Pacific Grove, has published a free self-guided walking tour featuring a number of our historic sites and structures. The guide is available on their websites: www.pacificgrove.org or www.pacificgroveheritage.org.

Beginnings

Pacific Grove began as a Piney Paradise[1] for the local Rumsen Ohlone Indians. The Ohlone lived here for over 7,000 years before the arrival of the Spaniards. They thrived on an abundance of fresh seafood and wild game in the year-round temperate climate. Marine life flourished and added to the rich environmental diversity of the area.

It was in 1542 that Juan Rodriguez Cabrillo first laid eyes on Pacific Grove, naming it Punta de los Pinos (Tip of the Pines), 60 years before Spanish explorer Sebastian Vizcaino named the Monterey Bay "Conde de Monterey."

In 1853, Cantonese Chinese fishermen established a fishing village, reaching from the present site of the Hopkins Marine Station to Point Alones, the present location of the Monterey Bay Aquarium. These Chinese fishermen were the first to commercialize the fishing industry in the Monterey Bay. Large Chinese "junks" carrying lanterns could be seen in the bay for more than 50 years. Tragically, a fire destroyed the village in 1906 and it was never rebuilt.

Point Pinos Lighthouse

1855

While the City of Monterey was already a bustling port-of-call in the 1880s, Pacific Grove remained quiet and unpopulated. Point Pinos Lighthouse was built in 1853 yet sat unused for two years, waiting for delivery of its Fresnel lens from France. Only in 1855 did the lighthouse begin to guide sailors through the fog to the port of Monterey. The lighthouse stood alone on the craggy coast for some 20 years before the construction of Lighthouse Avenue connected it to the Port of Monterey.

Although first maintained by lighthouse keepers who lived in the property's cottage, Point Pinos was automated in 1975. It now stands as the oldest continuously operating lighthouse on the Pacific Coast. The Lighthouse is open to the public.

[1] *A Piney Paradise (by the Monterey Bay) is the title of a book about Pacific Grove written by Lucy Neely McLane in 1952.*

Pacific Grove Retreat

In 1875, a Methodist minister in ill health was advised to spend time in a place with little temperature variation. J.W. Ross had been invited to camp on private land in the forest now known as Pacific Grove. He slept in a hammock among the pines and was soon cured of his aliments. He returned home to the San Francisco Bay Area and convinced his congregation that the area to the southwest of Monterey, with its mild weather, would be ideal for their annual summer retreat.

The Methodists persuaded landowner David Jacks to deed them approximately 100 acres along the Pacific Coast and named their governing organization the Pacific Grove Retreat Association. Every year, during Pacific Grove's summer season, tents sprang up amidst the pines and followers would gather to learn and worship for a few weeks.

In November 1879, after the summer campers had left the piney forest, Robert Louis Stevenson wandered into the deserted campgrounds and noted this experience in his book *The Old Pacific Capitol*:

After a while the woods began to open, the sea to sound nearer at hand. I came upon a road, and, to my surprise, a stile. A step or two farther, and, without leaving the woods, I found myself among trim houses. I walked through street after street, parallel and at right angles, paved with sward and dotted with trees, but still undeniable streets, and each with its name posted at the corner, as in a real town. . . . Facing down the main thoroughfare—"Central Avenue," as it was ticketed—I saw an open-air temple, with benches and sounding-board, as though for an orchestra. The houses were all tightly shuttered; there was no smoke, or sound but of the waves, no moving thing. I have never been in any place that seemed so dreamlike.

This is an historical photograph of what Robert Louis Stevenson might have seen on the day he wandered into the Pacific Grove Retreat during the winter of 1879.

Pacific Grove Retreat

It has been estimated that in 1880, 100 tents were in use during that summer's Chautauqua gathering. Those who stayed for the summer rented 30' X 60' lots from The Association, with wood framed, 10' X 12' X 6' tents of heavy canvas. Each had a painted wood floor; doors swung on hinges and came with a lock and key. Each tent came furnished with a wood stove, a bedstead with a spring mattress top, blankets, pillowcases, a tea table, a washstand and basin, and two chairs.

While most were content to enjoy the mild weather and tranquil forest in a comfortably furnished tent during the summer months, others had plans for something more permanent. Within just a few years, small board and batten cottages began to spring up amidst the trees. Many even used the thick canvas from the tents as insulation for their new summer homes—thus dictating the size of the finished cottage.

Elihu Beard House

1880

Five generations of the Beard family have owned this beautiful home, built by Elihu Beard as a summer family home in 1880. The original house stood on two lots, with a garden and croquet court where the driveway, garage, and backyard are located today. In the 1900s, the backyard shed was converted into a bedroom with a breezeway; the downstairs bathroom, the kitchen, and a third bedroom and bathroom on the second floor were updated. In the early 1950s, the front porch railing and planter bed were added. The Beard family continues to keep this house in prime historical condition.

Chautauqua Hall

1881

In 1879, Rev. John Heyl Vincent, a Methodist leader from New York, came to Pacific Grove and founded the West Coast Headquarters of the "Chautauqua Literary and Scientific Circle," a Methodist education movement that was highly popular in the late 19th and early 20th centuries.

In 1881, the Retreat Association built a permanent structure for its Chautauqua gatherings. Named after Chautauqua Lake, New York, where the first gatherings had been held, Chautauqua assemblies spread throughout rural America until the mid-1920s.

Pacific Grove's Chautauqua Hall became an active place, with education, entertainment, and plenty of preaching scheduled throughout the summer months. Its simple board and batten structure served the Retreat well, and, at the close of the Chautauqua season, the tent canvases were removed from their frames and stored in Chautauqua Hall throughout the winter months.

In the 1930s, the building was moved 25 feet to permit the widening of Central Avenue. During this period, the Hall was re-wired, re-plumbed, and re-shingled, and an extension was built on the rear of the building. For more than 100 years, the hall has remained an integral part of the community. Today, it serves as a meeting place for Boy Scouts, exercise and dance classes, special events, and private celebrations.

Railroad Brings New Arrivals

By 1885, Pacific Grove had become a destination on the Southern Pacific Railway's "Road of A Thousand Wonders," attracting thousands of visitors via train each summer. Some of these visitors took up permanent residence in The Grove. The wealthy chose to build their summer retreats in the style of the Victorian architecture of the day—Queen Anne Revival, with a few grand examples of Gothic Revival, Italianate, and even a tiny castle thrown in for diversity.

Everett Pomeroy House

1883
The Castle

The Castle stands tall overlooking Monterey Bay. Everett Pomeroy bought the lot in 1883 and, like many others, erected a tent cabin as part of the Retreat community. Later that year, he began construction on a permanent structure, first building the dining room and tower—the dining room's insulation made from the original tent. Other rooms were added over the years.

Pomeroy was a renowned author, composer, and organist. He modeled the tower on his family's 15th century castle in South Devon, England, the Berry Pomeroy Castle.

Retreat Cottages

Pacific Grove's less privileged were no less dignified. They dressed their wooden cottages in a Gothic Vernacular or what has been called Country Gothic style, with fretwork, gingerbread, fish scale shingles and other adornments.

These cottages were laid out with the living/gathering room up front and sleeping quarters in the rear. Most of these "retreat cottages" were without indoor plumbing until the turn of the 20th century.

Caroline Thornton House

1883

With its Carpenter Gothic overtones and Stick-style detailing, this tiny Victorian summer cottage had grand ambitions, considering its humble beginnings as one of the original tent houses in the Retreat. The home's broad front steps, blending into an open front porch, are one of its most distinctive features.

First Homesteaders

The Retreat's first homesteaders were quite sophisticated. With them, they brought such luxuries as porcelain chamber pots, stained glass, and worldly appointments such as imported furnishings and fine china. Old photos show that early Retreat tent campers spread carpets and served meals on elaborate dinnerware placed upon lace tablecloths.

Yet in Pacific Grove, it was moral rather than financial prosperity that was valued most highly. Cleanliness of the spirit and mind—as well as of the household—were of utmost importance. Therefore, women, while having great personal freedom in Pacific Grove, were often busy sweeping, dusting, and washing, in an effort to remain close to God and keep the neighbors from talking.

James J. Stevinson House

1883

This beautiful Carpenter Gothic was built as a smaller replica of James J. Stevinson's home in Stevinson, California, to be used as the family's summer retreat. The board and batten house is made of redwood, single-wall construction with bargeboard trim in the gables and decorative stickwork trim in the dormers. A porch wraps around two sides and is topped by a "widow's walk."

It is said that this property was the site of Pacific Grove's first wedding—that of Mr. Stevinson's sister-in-law.

Pacific Grove's First Church

1887

The Methodists may have founded Pacific Grove, but it was the Episcopalians who built the first church in The Grove in 1887.

St. Mary's-by-the-Sea Episcopal Church traces its English Gothic roots directly to its model in Bath, England. The church was enlarged in 1911 by splitting it down the center so that the oldest sections are now at the front and the back. The job was done under the free supervision of Lewis P. Hobart, the architect for San Francisco's massive Grace Cathedral.

Reminiscent of the ribbing of a ship's hull, the interior woodwork is natural pine, cedar, redwood, and walnut. A wealthy follower, Cyrus H. McCormick, donated the pair of stained glass "Lily" windows signed by Louis Comfort Tiffany.

The Methodists, encouraged by the building of St. Mary's, completed their own church in 1888. It sat proudly in the center of town until it was demolished in 1964. Its replacement now resides in the pines off Sunset Drive and 17 Mile Drive.

Founding of Pacific Grove

The Retreat area was officially incorporated as The City of Pacific Grove in 1889. At the time, some 1,300 permanent residents were building board and batten structures in place of their tents. Many of these tiny historic cottages in the original Retreat area on 16th, 17th, and 18th Streets, below Lighthouse Avenue still carry remnants of the original canvas tents inside.

Gosbey House

1887

J. F. Gosbey, a native of Nova Scotia, began building this Queen Anne manor house in 1886 and completed the original two-story Victorian in 1887. Its turret, variety of surface textures, and bay windows serve as prime examples of the style.

The Gosby House (with a slight variation of the original owner's name), fully restored and appointed with period antiques, is now an elegant bed & breakfast inn.

Honoring The Founding Fathers

Nearly a dozen Pacific Grove Retreat Association ministers were honored with their own street names: T. H. Sinex; Wesley Dennett; R. Bentley; M. C. Briggs; W. C. Evans; Otis Gibson; F. F. Jewell; and H. B. Heacock.

Street names, such as Bennett, Eardley, Olmsted, and Crocker, honor leaders in the Pacific Improvement Company. Yet others were named after community leaders and national heroes of the time that the City was being formed, such as Dewey, Spazier, and S.F.B. Morse.

William Lacy House

1888
Green Gables Inn

William Lacy's Queen Anne Revival, then called Ivy Terrace Hall, was one of the first to be built along the waterfront. Its huge bay windows take full advantage of its location, perched on the edge of the Monterey Bay. Remarkably, Lacy never lived in the home and, instead, allowed a family from his close social circle, that of Emma S. Murdoch and her daughter Penelope, to live in the home. He sold it to Emma in 1893 before heading off to inspect his mining interests. It is said that he perished at sea, in Mexican waters.

Today, the William Lacy House is a beautiful bed & breakfast inn filled with period antiques.

Pacific Grove Victorians

Building a grand Victorian towards the end of the 19th Century was a costly affair, with 1879 prices reaching upwards of $10,000. However, this tidy investment would likely have come with the newfangled indoor plumbing. These early "plunger closets" (toilets), bathtubs and washing sinks were most often encased in beautiful, hand-carved wood.

Charles Brown House

1888

Charles Brown built this property just north of its present location, to which it was moved sometime between 1916 and 1918. While this property is fairly large, house moving was a very common occurrence during this era—both in Pacific Grove and elsewhere in California. This two-story Carpenter's Gothic features Eastlake detailing such as fish scale shingles and three-pointed gables.

The house underwent various adaptations and was even divided into three separate living quarters in the late 1950s. Finally, in 1976, it was fully restored and returned to its original single-family use, as it remains today.

Pacific Grove Heritage Society's
Ketcham's Barn

1891

Ketcham's Barn has been home to the Heritage Society of Pacific Grove since 1981. It had been built 90 years earlier in 1891, soon after Joseph H. Ketcham bought the property from Mrs. I. A. Hill of Salinas. Its third owner, E. Cooke, used to keep his horse and buggy there. The City leased the Barn to the five-year-old Heritage Society in return for the Society's promise to restore and maintain it. The restoration preserved the character of the original barn, a 24-foot square, unpainted board and batten building. Replacing the original hayloft is the interior second story that serves as the Society's office and archive. Downstairs is a small museum, displaying photographs and artifacts. Ketcham's Barn is open to the public on Saturdays.

The Centrella

1892

Originally named Centrella Cottage, this two-story Victorian was constructed for use as a boarding house in a beach cottage style. Shortly after opening, The Centrella was dubbed "the largest, most commodious and pleasantly located private boarding house in The Grove" in the newspapers of the time.

The structure had a major face-lift in 1981, when the exterior was restored to its original grandeur and its facilities upgraded. Now, more than 100 years later, The Centrella continues to serve visitors to Pacific Grove, operating as a bed & breakfast inn. This property is listed on the National Historic Register.

Turn of the Century

The late 1800s were a remarkable time for Pacific Grove. The area was a well-known destination for the rich and powerful, hosting not one, but three, Presidents (Harrison in 1891; Roosevelt in 1896; and McKinley in 1901) in just ten years' time.

Building was booming, and in 1898, the first electric streetlight was lit in The Grove.

Trimmer Hill

1893

Dr. Oliver Smith Trimmer had this grand Queen Anne mansion built by George Quentel and Abraham Lee in 1893. Dr. Trimmer, a surgeon, was also the first mayor of Pacific Grove. The home was also the residence of Knut Hovden, owner of the cannery that was to become the Monterey Bay Aquarium.

The home, which sat on a large piece of property, took on the name "Trimmer Hill" in the 1930s, when it became a boarding house. It has been returned to a single-family dwelling and has retained a number of unique, historic adornments, such as the imported, carved elephant hide wainscoting in the dining room.

This is a perfect example of the Queen Anne style, featuring Eastlake detailing, romantic turret towers, angular bay windows, an arched entryway and corbelled brick chimneys. Trimmer Hill is the only private residence in Pacific Grove on the National Register of Historic Places.

A Bustling Seaside Community

Even before the turn of the 20th Century, Pacific Grove had built a bustling seaside business community, attracting shoppers and diners from Monterey and beyond. Visitors came by train, trolley, buggy, and foot.

In the early 1890s, downtown Pacific Grove had three grocery stores, a dry goods store, an ice cream parlor, a candy factory, a bakery, a sporting goods store, a clothing store and a shoe store, not to mention a millinery, a pharmacy, and an Indian Relics Trading Post.

Victorian Corner

1893

Victorian Corner started out as an Indian trading post, selling everything from seashells to pottery, from barbed wire to square head copper nails. The architecture of Victorian Corner has been unchanged since it was built. The high ceilings, beautiful windows, stained glass and exterior trim make this building one of Pacific Grove's finest examples of early Victorian architecture. The Aliotti Family have been the caretakers of this beautiful building for over 40 years. They opened their Sicilian-style restaurant, The Victorian Corner, in 1977.

Dr. Andrew Hart House

❧

1894

This grand Queen Anne manor house has long hosted a business on its first floor, often combined with family living quarters in its upper stories. The tradition began with the original owner, Dr. Andrew Jackson Hart, who built the house and practiced medicine on the ground floor while his family lived upstairs. His son, Dr. Frank R. Hart, followed suit. The tradition continues today, with an elegantly appointed Victorian Tea Room and event space downstairs and a residence upstairs.

One of the finest examples of Queen Anne architecture on the Monterey Peninsula, Dr. Hart's former home is embellished by a round turret featuring a witch's cap; elaborate stick work, spindles and brackets; diamond, triangle, and oval windows; and stained glass. A stained glass window honoring Dr. Hart can be found over the front door.

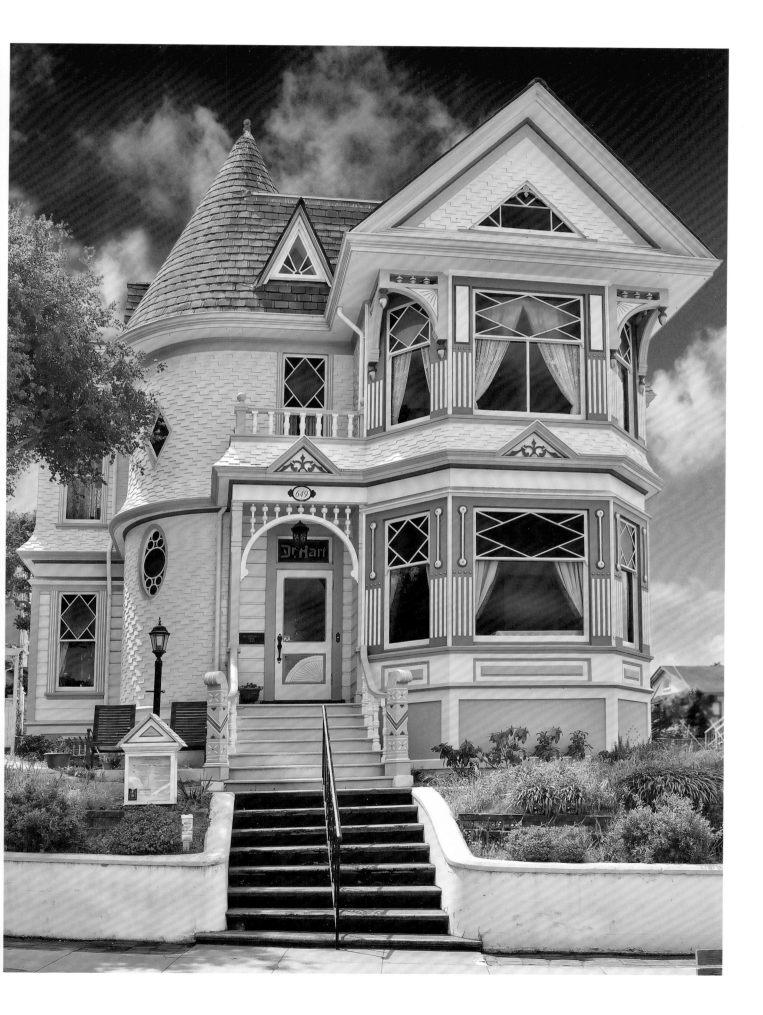

Then & Now

Dr. Sinex House

1885

Then & Now

Dr. Sinex House

2016

Then & Now

Methodist Church

1891

Then & Now

Methodist Church

2016

Then & Now

Lovers Point

1914

Then & Now

Lovers Point

2016

Lizzie M. McKee House

❧

1903

This charming Queen Anne Style cottage stands on one of Pacific Grove's oldest streets. Its facade is rich in historic details, including: carved barge boards, a rosette in the center of the shingled front gable, and brackets on the front porch.

Originally owned by Lizzie M. McKee, this property has had several owners since. The current owners have lovingly restored the cottage and are active members of the Heritage Society.

Pacific Grove Victorian Influences

As Pacific Grove moved toward the 20th Century, families took up full time residence and homes became much more elaborately furnished. While Monterey residences reflected the bounty of the port filled with goods from Asia and Spain, Pacific Grove residents were more inclined to decorate in the fashion of Queen Victoria.

A number of these historic homes still hold the original woodwork. Some even boast the original light fixtures and a few have miraculously preserved the original plumbing fixtures—all while conditioning the spaces for modern living.

Toad Hall

1904

Toad Hall was built in 1904 on a street then called Grove Street. The Monterey and Pacific Grove Electric Railway once ran right past its front door.

Today, this historic home is affectionately called Toad Hall—a name chosen by its owners from "The Wind in the Willows." The owners removed asbestos siding and restored the historic wooden kitchen counters, as well as the period wainscoting and wallpaper. The home boasts its original light fixtures in the front room.

Sara Ann Uren House

❧

1904

The tiny cottage, long known as The Pink House, was built in 1904 using a three-room tent as the form. This fine example of an early Retreat home—which began as a tent, grew with the times, and continues to evolve— has been featured in many publications and advertisements.

The current owners refurbished the existing structure and added a second story at the far back of the house. Evidence of the three tents, which first comprised the home, can be seen in the layout of the original Douglas fir floors.

Women In Pacific Grove

Pacific Grove has a history of being a woman-friendly community. In fact, a good number of the Heritage Home Plaques feature women's names, even though these women were often married when the home was purchased. Many women came to Pacific Grove to make a better life for themselves.

Emily Williams & Lillian Palmer House

1904

Two such women, Emily Williams and Lillian Palmer, arrived in Pacific Grove at the turn of the 20th century. Williams was a pioneering female architect who was active at a time when very few women were able to enter the profession. The two women built two homes in Pacific Grove, completing all the work themselves. This accomplishment received attention from the press and soon became a tourist attraction. As a result of these successes, Williams went on to design at least a dozen more homes before retiring.

D. T. Welch House

1905

This property has had a rich and colorful history over the past 100-plus years. In addition to being the private residence of the Welch family, it has been both a boarding house known for its loud, legendary parties and a dental office.

However, it may be most notable for having housed the offices of Gary Kildall's high-tech phenomenon, Digital Research—the company that created the software precursor to MicroSoft. The system created in this Pacific Grove home in the 1970s is considered by many to be the forerunner of the software systems that run the majority of the world's personal computers today. A plaque commemorating this home's historic occupancy was dedicated in 2014.

The home has been restored to its original character, utilizing original doors, windows, and light fixtures throughout, including push-button light switches.

Frank E. Buck House

1905

Frank Buck, an early prominent businessman and civic leader in The Grove, built this Queen Anne Manor on the corner of Pine and Forest Avenues. The local paper announced, "The foundation has been laid for F.L. Buck's handsome new residence. The plans, drawn by architect Robert Glass, show that the structure will be an imposing one and an ornament to that part of the city."

The structure fell into disrepair in the 1970s and was used as a "flop house" of sorts until it was sold and completely restored in 1985 to become the Pacific Grove Inn. It was placed on the National Historic Register in 1986.

End of the Victorian Reign

By 1900, Queen Victoria's reign over Pacific Grove architecture was coming to an end. New manor houses of Neo-Classic design, with imposing Tuscan columns (smooth and rounded) and full pediments, began to replace scrolls and spindles. Then came the layered box design of American Foursquare and Colonial Revival, with its Saltbox roofs. All of these architectural styles can still be found in Pacific Grove.

Wallace Brown House

1907

This home sits on the western end of the expansive Pine Avenue. Expanded and updated at the end of the last century, it is a beautiful example of Dutch Colonial architecture. The unique gambrel roof line has two slopes on each side, with the lower slope having the steeper pitch. This unusual roofline gives the interior spaces a grand open feeling.

Although its original owner owned the property for only one year, the home remains the Wallace Brown House in perpetuity.

New Era of Pacific Grove

Times had changed so dramatically that the final Chautauqua gathering was held in Pacific Grove in 1926. By this time, many artists and writers had been drawn to The Grove's beautiful landscapes and quiet atmosphere. Writer John Steinbeck lived in Pacific Grove from 1930 to 1936. It has been said that those were his happiest years. Steinbeck mentions his new home in the book *Cannery Row* in the now famous line: "Carmel by the Sea, Pacific Grove by God, and Monterey by the Smell."

William Adam House

1907

The house's first owner, William Constable Adam, was a Scottish-born oil and watercolor painter who moved to Pacific Grove in 1906 and lived the rest of his life in this romantic cottage. His work is included in the Smithsonian Institution collection.

The cottage was purchased in 2005, and the new owners restored the exterior to its former vintage glory—from a new foundation on up—while remodeling the inside to meet the family's contemporary needs. The owners used antiques throughout, including lighting, window latches, bathtubs and fixtures.

Pacific Grove Bungalows

Pacific Grove was a real estate haven at the turn of the 20th century, when Craftsman style architecture was coming of age. One could buy plans for small bungalows through the mail for as little as 90 cents. Kit homes were all the rage, ordered from manufacturers such as Sears & Roebuck and delivered by truck. The buyer needed to supply only the land and the foundation. Aladdin Co. advertised a $1.00 discount for every knothole found in its kits.

Pacific Grove has a number of kit homes scattered throughout town. A small four-room bungalow kit cost $419, excluding a bathroom, while a grand Victorian style home with five to six rooms, including a bathroom, could cost as much as $1,200 or more.

James C. Brown House

1910

Other than the name of the original owner, little is known about this property's first 60 years. Yet in the 1970s, it was the home of the owners of Tillie Gort's restaurant, a Pacific Grove institution during the City's bohemian era. At that time, there was an open-air toilet at the top of the stairs.

The current owners have completely refurbished the house. The original wainscoting in the living room and dining room has been continued throughout the house, and the fireplace mantle has been restored to its former glory, with its original hand-painted inserts.

Asilomar Conference Grounds

Merrill Hall
1913

By the turn of the 20th Century, Pacific Grove's architecture also included many fine examples of Craftsman bungalows, and the concept of shingled siding had become more popular. It was around this time (1913-1928) that famed architect Julia Morgan designed many of the buildings that still grace the Asilomar Conference Grounds. While they were originally designed to shelter the women of the YWCA, the property is now open to the public as part of the California State Park system.

Merrill Hall, the Social Hall (now the main administration building), the Chapel, and a handful of other shingle-and-stone structures were all designed by Julia Morgan and serve as excellent examples of the era's Arts & Crafts Movement. Morgan is best known for her later work for William Randolph Hearst at San Simeon's Hearst Castle.

In 1987, the 11 remaining Julia Morgan-designed buildings at Asilomar were designated National Historic Landmarks.

Holman's Department Store

1924

Rensselaer Luther Holman opened his first dry goods store in Pacific Grove in 1891. In 1918, his son, Wilford Rensselaer Holman, purchased the lot that formerly housed the El Carmelo Hotel to build Holman's Department Store, one of the largest retail buildings in the county at the time of its construction. The stories say that he added more floors to keep men at work during the depression. Holman's grew to become the largest independently owned and operated department store between Los Angeles and San Francisco, filling mail orders from around the world. It was the founder's son, W.R. Holman, who masterminded the building of the portion of Highway 68 from Pacific Grove to Carmel Hill, now Holman Highway, in an effort to make the department store more accessible.

The internationally acclaimed writer John Steinbeck purchased his writing supplies at Holman's and wrote of it in his famous book *Cannery Row.*

In 2016, this structure, now simply referred to as Holman's, was in the process of being converted into a multiuse building with townhouses upstairs and retail on the street level. It serves as an example of early modern architecture, with hints of the original Art Deco influences.

Spanish Influences

By 1926, you could purchase a newly built, four-room home for about $3,500. The home came complete with a fireplace, hardwood floors, a large kitchen and bath. All this for just $350.00 down and $35.00 per month.

While neighboring Monterey holds true Spanish Colonial roots, it was a more modest Pueblo Revival that became popular in Pacific Grove between 1915 and 1930. Charming examples, with stucco siding, arched, bull-nosed features, and clay tile roofs, are preserved throughout the city.

Pueblo Revival

1926

These three charming examples of Pueblo Revival each has its own distinct personality. All three feature flat roofs with low, parapet walls and arched window accents in the entry porches. These tiny cottages were to resemble adobes found in the Southwest but seem to fit very well in the seaside town of Pacific Grove.

Then & Now

Holman House

1890

Then & Now

Holman House

Stuccoed in 1924

2016

Then & Now

Architect, William H. Weeks

1905

Then & Now

Architect, William H. Weeks

2016

Then & Now

Osborne House

1910

Then & Now

Osborne House

2016

Lovers Point Beach

The area known as Lovers Point Beach underwent several variations over the past century. A series of public bathhouses were built—the first in 1875 and the last in 1949. **In 1904, a Japanese Tea House was built on the waterfront. In 1909, a permanent pier was added.** Ladies stopped there for tea and a visit to the Lovers Point Dahlia Gardens, which won an international horticulture Gold Medal award in 1915. Although the Tea House closed in 1924, Lovers Point continued to evolve. Starting in 1949, four beachfront restaurants were built, each one replacing the last. Glass-bottomed swan boat tours began in the 1890s and continued for nearly 80 years. A replica of a swan boat at the beach entrance still welcomes beachgoers. Today, Lovers Point remains a destination for relaxation and celebration, with water sports, picnic tables, and a restaurant for fine dining.

Feast of Lanterns

1879

Lovers Point Beach is the home of a century-old celebration, The Feast of Lanterns. This event began as the closing ceremony for the Methodists' annual Chautauqua retreat. Participants would gather with lit lanterns and make a procession to Lovers Point Beach to announce the closing of the season. Lanterns were hung from street lamps and Victorian porches.

Over the years, the event evolved into today's celebration, which consists of a full week of festivities, including a pet parade down Lighthouse Avenue and a dance at the historic Chautauqua Hall. The week-long event culminates with a day of celebration at the beach, ending with a play based on the story created for the English china pattern The Blue Willow. However, instead of the English version, in which the lovers transform into doves, the Pacific Grove version transforms the lovers into Monarch Butteries to forever fly free. A fireworks display signals the close of the celebration.

Monarch Butterflies

Even during the earliest religious gatherings, people took notice of the large numbers of Monarch Butterflies overwintering amidst the pines. This annual migration is so unique that Pacific Grove carries the nickname, "Butterfly Town, U.S.A."

Pacific Grove entrepreneur, W.R. Holman, was once asked what Pacific Grove looked like when he first arrived in 1888. He responded:

And then the butterflies, like the butterflies that are here now, they were here in, oh, much greater quantities than they are now. They would settle on pine trees. The trees that they selected, you couldn't see any foliage hardly at all-just one solid mass of hanging butterflies in great cones...And then on nice warm, sunny days, the butterflies would be all through the air, just thousands of them...

Today, Pacific Grove offers nature lovers a unique experience when thousands upon thousands of Monarch butterflies visit from October through February each year. While these beautiful insects can be seen throughout town, a great number of them gather in the trees just off Ridge Road, in what is now officially designated the Monarch Grove Sanctuary.

In 1939, Pacific Grove drew international attention when it passed an ordinance making it a misdemeanor to molest a butterfly. Today, the Pacific Grove Police Department still enforces this regulation with a $1,000 fine.

It was also in 1939 that the first ever Butterfly Parade was held. In its earliest years, organizers would release hundreds of Monarch butterflies into the air at the launch of the parade. To this day, every first Saturday in October, the children of Pacific Grove dress as Monarch butterflies and parade through town.

Pacific Grove is also known as "A Piney Paradise." The Monterey Pines (Pinus radiata), which grow abundantly throughout the town, are found in only three places in the world: California's Central Coast, Mexico's Guadalupe Island and Cedros Island. The Monarchs are often found clustered in these tall evergreens.

Pacific Grove's Magic Carpet

∽

Pacific Grove's Coastal Recreation Trail is on a beautiful stretch of land that starts at the edge of the Pacific Ocean near Asilomar Beach and travels east past rolling white dunes and wind-swept cypress trees towards Lovers Point and Monterey.

At Lovers Point Beach, every spring, a brilliant, hot pink "Magic Carpet" covers the rocky coastline. In 1938, Hayes Perkins, at 60 years old, single-handedly planted "the Magic Carpet. " At that time, the point was covered with poison oak, to which he was immune. Watching the children run through the thickets, he took it upon himself to remove the native tyrant. Then, with his own funds and labor, he planted and maintained his African Scarlet Aloe cuttings, adding accents of calla lilies, geraniums, and pelargoniums as he moved down the coastline. This area, one of Pacific Grove's most photographed, is named Perkins Park in his honor.

Acknowledgements

We would like to thank the following individuals and organizations for their help producing this picture book for the residents and visitors of Pacific Grove.

Photographer, Craig Riddell
The Heritage Society of Pacific Grove
Jean Anton, The Heritage Society of Pacific Grove
The City of Pacific Grove
Tad Burness & his book, The Vintage House Book
Tom Stevens

Pat Hathaway's California Views

Paul, Domenic & Mary Alioti
Betty Beard
The Beacon House
Bill & Helen Bluhm
The Bridge Restoration Ministry
Ed & Vanessa Bredthauer
Gwen & John Callan
Joe & Linda Donofrio
Four Sisters Inns
First United Methodist Church
Nina Grannis
Christine & Marc Griffith
Barry & Jan Jeffries
Carol & Michael Mazur
Jeanne Mills
Michael & Ann Mulvihill
Amrish G. & Jignasa Patel
Tricia & Tony Perault
Carl & Donna Stewart
St. Mary's By-The-Sea
Donna Deaver Tuma
Jim & Kathy Turley
United Methodist Church
Kerry Walker
Craig Johnson & Marlene Williamson
Xi & Brien Wilson

A Very Special Thank You to Don Beals,
of The Heritage Society of Pacific Grove
for his valuable assistance.